Text © 2020 Matt Brennan
Illustrations © Debbie Armes

Text set in Noteworthy
Display text set in Snell Roundhand and
American Typewritter

Illustrations created in colored pencil
Incidental illustrations and effects created in Photoshop

Printed and bound in the United States of America
First Printing ---
Published by Ingram Content Group, La Vergne, TN, USA
ISBN: 978-0-578-72366-2

The Old Racist Cat

Written by Matt Brennan

Illustrated by Debbie Armes

And now I will tell you about an old, racist cat.

He's brittle. He's boney. But somehow still fat.

His faded orange fur hangs off him like the rug

Of a windy, wet, bald guy I once knew, named Doug.

Patchy and petulant, Hutch is his name.

No one's quite sure from whence he did came.

But Hutch? He just don't like the tone of your skin.

If you'll spare me a minute, his tale I'll begin.

It started with the Irish, the gingers next door.

He'll spend all his years trying to settle that score.

On a bright, pleasant day Hutch had found a sun beam,

On top of a wall, where he could lie and daydream.

Until Sally O'Toole a dim shadow
did cast.

She had stopped there to pet him.
But he hadn't asked.

So now he knew that they could
not coexist.

Yes, since that dark day,
that pussy's been pissed

Speaking of pee, that's his favorite weapon.

He'll watch and then whiz in a spot that you'll step in.

Especially when someone's skin color's brown.

He's been marking turf up all over the town.

At Javier's house, and then on to Juan.

Camila was next, and then Esteban.

Of course this all started with an act so unfair.

Carla had two burritos. That she wouldn't share!

One time there came
just the cutest young troop

Of girl scouts with cookies
here onto my stoop.

Hutch went out to greet them
and thought they were splendid.

'Til one started sneezing
and Hutch was offended.

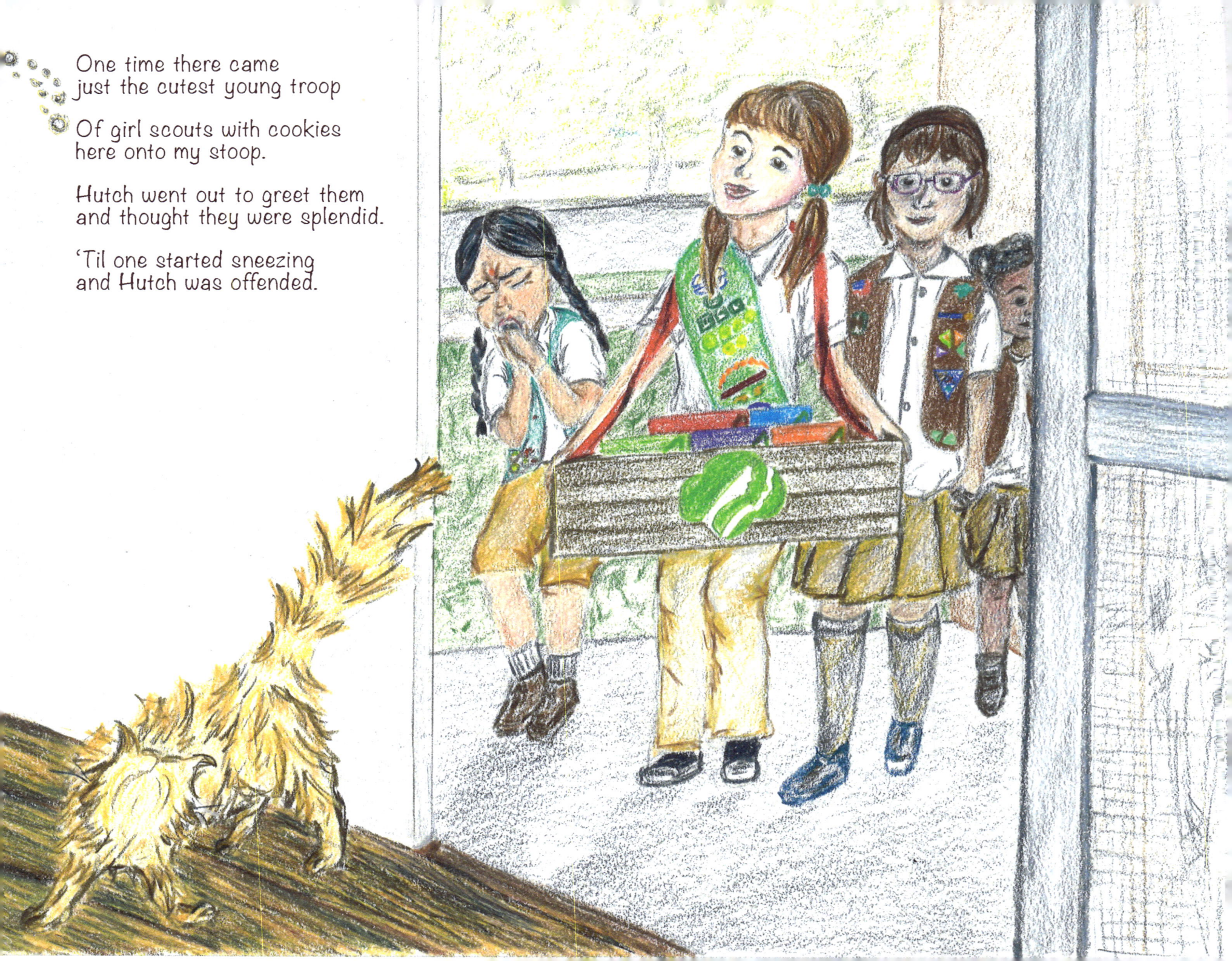

That Indian girl
did not see it coming.

As she made her deliveries,
the war drums were drumming.

All of her customers
found something askew.

Not boxes of cookies,
but boxes of poo.

Despite those dull eyes that no longer see faces,

He can spot a Samoan from five hundred paces.

And that nose that turns up at all kinds of chow?

It seems to smell Arabs. I'm not sure quite how.

He can catch a Scottish brogue
from a mile or so away,

Yet doesn't hear me call him
at the end of the day.

He's got a sixth sense
for when gypsies are near,

But they've got it too,
so they all steer clear.

Now if your name happens to be Rebecca Soo,

Then you can be sure that this old cat hates you.

And really most anyone of the Asian persuasion.

'Cuz for him it's a fairly simple equation.

Rebecca once stepped on his tail at a brunch.

Then while eating her eggs she heard a slight crunch.

It seems that the tabby thought her meal was quite dull.

So he added a skeleton and a little mouse skull.

My maid named Anouk once vacuumed too near.

So Cheeseheads were added to the list in that year.

According to Hutch, Anouk looks like a cow.

He declines to say Meee and gives only Owww.

Italians he'll snub. No, he'll not say not a word.

But later on their doorstep they'll find a dead bird.

He's seen The Godfather about seventeen times.

And he likes the symbolism of horse-head-y crimes.

Bananas and Frogs, Cabbage eater and Limey.

Hillbillies and Half-Breeds, plus folks who are whiny.

White Trash and Taffies and Gringos, oh my!

These are just some of those he would decry.

He hisses at Haitians and growls at Jews.

Louder and louder and louder he mews!

Scratching and clawing at legs like cat posts.

And then there's black people. He hates them the most.

Three things I can tell you about Hutch with his foe:
Sometimes he'll go fast and sometimes he'll go slow,
And sometimes he waits and plays the long game,
So's a lonely Kenyan man won't know why he came.

He'll eat that man's food.
Keep him company, too.

Snuggle up on the couch
when he seems to feel blue.

And then disappear
for three days at a time.

Which worries the man.
Yes, that is his crime.

So that is the cat. His tale has been told.

I know he's a monster, but he's also quite old.

He's set in his ways. He cannot be taught

To change his opinions, to be what he's not.

Yet I've grown rather fond of the biased old coot.

And he seems to tolerate me now, to boot.

Now how can that be, my skin black as anyone's?

Well ...

I suppose that he thinks that I'm one of the good ones.
———

Matt Brennan

Lives in Burbank, CA with a used, black cat named Bagheera that he obtained when her original family moved to Japan (she likes him better anyway). He enjoys poking fun at pretty much everything, including touchy subjects. This is his second book.

Debbie Armes

Loves animals of all kinds, especially ones with character. With her husband, she corrals four kids and their 6 pets. She has always loved to draw, tell stories, read stories, and learn. She lives in North Hollywood with her family and enjoys teaching squirrelly second graders.